The Wheelie Time Machine

Contents

The Baby	3
The Wheelie-Beelie	8
When Grandma was a Little Girl	16
The Thunderstorm	25
The Wheelie-Beelie Bomb Race	32
Grandma	41
Polly Again	45

Written by Eric Johns
Illustrated by Alan Marks

Collins Educational
An imprint of HarperCollinsPublishers

The Baby

The wheelie-beelie charged madly down the garden. Its wheels banged against the bricks at the edge of the path. It seemed to have come alive. Emma dug her nails into the wooden seat to stay on. The freezing night air poked icily through her pyjamas.

All around her there were flashes of lightning and crashes of thunder. Each one was brighter and louder than the last. They seemed to be chasing her. Flash-crash! In the street. Flash-crash! In the next door garden. FLASH-CRASH! The last one hurled itself out of the sky straight at the wheelie-beelie.

Emma screamed. In front of her was the garden rockery. But it had changed. A black hole, like the mouth of a cave, had opened in its side and there were steps going down into the earth. The wheelie-beelie was heading straight for them. It bounced down the first one and tipped forward. Emma was thrown into the darkness. She screamed again. Behind her there was the most deafening roar she had ever heard. The whole world shook. Everything was falling on top of her. She struggled to escape but she was trapped. Where was she? she asked herself. How had she got there?

✼ ✼ ✼

It all began on the day her dad collected her from school.

"Where's Mum?" Emma asked.

"She's gone into the maternity unit," her dad said, starting the car.

"Is the baby coming?" Emma asked excitedly.

"Well," her dad said slowly, "we're not sure."

"You said the baby would be born when Mummy went there," Emma answered him.

"It will be," her dad told her. "But we're not sure when."

"Then why's Mummy gone there?" Emma wanted to know.

"She went to the doctor at the clinic this morning," her dad explained, "and he said she must go into the maternity unit to wait for the baby." Her dad smiled at her in the driving mirror.

Emma had a tight, fluttery feeling in her tummy. "Is something the matter?"

"There's nothing to worry about," her dad said, smiling again. But she *was* worried. Her dad saw her face in the mirror.

"Do you know where we're going?" he asked. She knew he was trying to make her think about something else.

"I'm going to Mrs Cook's house," she said.

"No." He laughed because she looked surprised. "You're going to Grandma and Grandpa's."

As soon as he said that, she felt *sure* there was something wrong. Her mum had told her what would happen when the baby was born. Mrs Cook, their neighbour, would look after her, while Dad took Mum into the maternity unit. Dad would come home after the baby was born, and Mum would bring the baby home the next day. She wasn't going to be away for long. That's what had happened when Emma's friend's mum had her baby. Now something was wrong.

"There's something the matter, isn't there?" Emma said again.

"Everything's all right," her dad told her. But his smile wasn't the same as usual, and Emma wasn't fooled. Why wouldn't he tell her what was going on? If Mum had been there, *she* would have told her.

Her dad drove to Grandma and Grandpa's house. "I'll see you in the morning," he promised her. "Be a good girl." They all waved as he drove away.

"Everything will be all right," Grandpa said.

"She knows that," Grandma said in her reliable no-nonsense voice. But they both looked worried, and they smiled too much.

Emma felt strange and alone.

The Wheelie-Beelie

Usually Emma liked her grandma's house.

It was old and very tall and in the middle of a row of other houses which were all exactly the same. Inside there were lots of dark corners, and it had a musty smell because some rooms were never used.

After her dad had gone, Emma went into the kitchen at the back where Grandma was making the tea. At home Emma and her mum and dad had their meals in the kitchen, but Grandma's kitchen was too tiny for a table.

"No room to swing a cat in here," Grandma complained. She always said that. Emma had a picture in her head of Grandma, in her apron, holding a cat by its tail and trying to swing it round and banging its head on the kitchen walls. "That's cruel," she told her.

"Not that sort of cat," Grandma said. "A cat o'nine tails."

"I've never seen a cat with more than one tail," Emma replied.

Grandma turned round and nearly fell over her. "Go on down the garden and get under your grandpa's feet, Miss Cleverclogs, or I'll never have your tea ready."

Grandma always called her Cleverclogs when she argued. Emma went out. The garden wasn't really a

garden. At least it was not like her garden at home. There was a path made from bluey-black bricks which stretched from the kitchen door to the back gate. Along one side of it was a narrow flower border.

Down the other side were Grandpa's workshed and a wooden pigeon coop where his racing pigeons lived.

At the very bottom of the garden was a big rockery, taller than Emma, which she was allowed to climb. It was her favourite game when she was there. She would pretend she was climbing a mountain to her secret den at the top behind some bushes. The leaves hid her, but she could usually see Grandma through the kitchen window and hear Grandpa talking to his pigeons.

Emma found Grandpa in his workshed. He was screwing something onto a piece of wood.

"What are you doing?" Emma asked.

"Wait a minute and you will see," he said, and winked at her.

"Is it something for me?"

"Could be," he grunted, pushing down hard on the screwdriver.

"What is it?"

He lifted a strange-looking thing off his workbench. It was a plank of wood with a loop of string nailed on it, and underneath there were four legs with silvery wheels. Emma thought she had

seen the wheels before.

"There you are," Grandpa said. "It's all yours."

"What is it?" Emma asked again.

"What is it?" Grandpa pretended to be surprised at the question. "What is it?" he repeated. "You're having me on, aren't you?"

"If you don't want to tell me," Emma said, pretending not to care, "I think I'll go and have a look at my den."

"Ah, well. If that's what you want to do," Grandpa said, "I'll just put the wheelie-beelie up on the bench out of the way."

"Is it a wheelie-beelie?" Emma asked.

"Now you're asking," Grandpa said. "Follow me."

He led the way up the narrow path to the kitchen door and placed the wheelie-beelie on the path.

"On you get," he said.

Emma sat on it and held the string.

"Lift up your feet and I'll give you a push," Grandpa told her.

She went clattering over the bricks. The path sloped and she kept going right down to her rockery mountain. She came to a halt, got off and pulled the wheelie-beelie back to Grandpa.

"It's a go-cart on stilts," she told him.

"Go-cart, eh?" Grandpa said, scratching his head. "When I was a boy we called them wheelie-beelies. Everyone had one made out of old bits and pieces."

"Those wheels used to be under the television," Emma said, suddenly remembering.

"When we got rid of the old telly, I kept them. They seemed too good to throw away." He bent down.

"Do you think you can find a use for a wheelie-beelie?"

"Oh, yes." Emma gave him a kiss. "I'll ride it and move things about on it."

"I thought you could do with something to play with while you're here."

Grandpa's words reminded her why she was there. "When can I see Mum?" Emma asked.

"I don't know, love. A day or two. Not long." He smiled. "Don't worry. You have a ride."

Emma knew that the wheelie-beelie was supposed

to stop her worrying about her mum and the baby. She pushed herself off and rode down the path.

After a few tries she got the speed just right, so that she could go as fast as possible without crashing into the rockery. When she got tired of that she climbed the rockery mountain to her den and crouched down behind the bushes. She looked at the backs of the houses in the row and wondered how long before she could see her mum again. She tried to think what could be the matter.

The baby was late coming, Emma knew that because she had been waiting for the day when she would be born. On that day the baby would have her nothing-years-old-birthday. Emma had thought that was funny, but remembering it now didn't cheer her up.

She watched Grandpa's pigeons fly round in circles and land on the roof of their coop in a neat line. When she helped Grandpa clean them out she held the birds in her hands and felt their hearts fluttering.

When Grandma was a Little Girl

Grandma opened the kitchen door and shouted, "Tea-time!"

Emma climbed down her rockery mountain. She sat astride the wheelie-beelie and scooted it two-legged up to the top of the path.

Grandpa followed Emma into the kitchen singing, "Polly, put the kettle on, we'll all have tea."

"Wash your hands and sit down," Grandma said sharply. "Never mind singing."

Emma and Grandpa washed their hands at the kitchen sink while Grandma grumbled about them being in the way. Then they went and sat in their places in the small dining-room and waited for Grandma.

Emma's chair faced the window and she could see her rockery mountain. She liked having tea at Grandma's. It was a proper meal with ham and cheese and tea-cakes and jelly and evaporated milk as well as bread and butter.

Emma half closed her eyes and looked hard at Grandpa. "You and Grandma," she said slowly, "are like Jack Sprat and his wife."

"Oh," Grandpa said, looking at her seriously, "and why's that?"

"Because you're thin and Grandma's fattish," Emma said, not quite wanting to call Grandma fat, "and between you everything gets eaten."

"I shouldn't let Grandma hear you call her fattish," he whispered, glancing at the door to the kitchen as if he was frightened of Grandma.

"What was Jack Sprat's wife called?" Emma asked him suddenly.

"Mrs Sprat," he replied straightaway.

"Her *other* name I mean," Emma sighed.

"Mrs Polly-put-the-kettle-on Sprat."

"You don't know," Emma said with a snort.

"Here, you two, eat your tea," Grandma interrupted, plonking a teapot on the table and sitting down.

They ate until all the plates were empty.

"Like Jack Sprat and his wife," Emma whispered.

After tea Emma helped clear the table. She was always more helpful at Grandma's, but she didn't know why. Grandma didn't have a dishwasher so Emma did the drying up. She was quiet, thinking about her mum again.

When they had finished Grandma sat down in her comfortable chair in the dining-room. "Thank goodness that's over for another day," she said with a sigh.

Emma sat on the floor next to her chair. "Tell me about when you were a little girl," she begged, putting on her sweetest voice. If she could get Grandma talking, she could put off going to bed.

"I know what you're up to, young lady," Grandma said. "I wasn't born yesterday."

"When *were* you born?" Emma asked.

"A long time ago, and it's still your bedtime," Grandma replied.

"Were there dinosaurs when you were little?" Emma asked.

"Don't be cheeky, or it's off to bed right now."

"What did you look like?"

"I had fair hair like you, and blue eyes. But I wasn't as tall, and I didn't wear jeans."

"Did you have TV?" Emma leaned against Grandma's chair to be more comfortable.

"Well, it had been invented, but no-one had one until I was a lot older than you are," Grandma said. "When I was your age the war was on, and there was only the radio to listen to."

"Was the war exciting?" Emma asked.

"No. I didn't like it because we never had enough sweets or any oranges or bananas, and my dad, that's your great-grandpa – you never knew him – was away in the army, and I didn't see him for one whole year." Grandma had a far-away look on her face as if she was looking at things Emma couldn't see.

"What games did you play?" Emma asked.

"I remember one thing we played which I haven't seen for years," Grandma said, nodding at the memory. "Every Easter-time all the children used to be given new whips and tops."

"I've got a humming top," Emma said.

"These were little, coloured wooden tops, and you had to whip them to make them spin."

"Did you have a lot of friends?" Emma asked.

"About the usual number, I suppose. But," Grandma lowered her voice almost to a whisper, "I had one very special friend."

"Tell me about her," Emma said, looking up at her

grandma excitedly.

"She was a secret friend," Grandma went on. "No-one else knew about her."

"Was she real?" Emma asked.

"She was real to me," Grandma nodded and smiled. "We used to ride down the path on my wheelie-beelie, just like you this afternoon. My wheelie-beelie had pram wheels so it went even faster than yours, and we were always crashing. But my secret friend never hurt herself."

"She wasn't real, was she?" Emma asked again.

"I suppose not," Grandma smiled. "But she was once. Just once."

"When was that?" Emma asked eagerly.

"I think that's enough of that nonsense," Grandpa said sharply, poking his head around the door.

Emma jumped. She had forgotten he was there.

"It's long past Emma's bedtime," he added, nodding at the clock on the mantelpiece.

Emma said goodnight, and was taken upstairs by Grandma. She didn't try to argue.

The house had two flights of stairs. On the first floor was the bathroom, Grandma and Grandpa's bedroom and a spare room. On the second floor there was one big room which was as wide as the house. Emma always wanted this room when she stayed because she thought it was exciting having a room which had a window on the street side of the house and another on the garden side.

"Tell me more about your special friend," Emma asked Grandma, as soon as she was in bed.

"I pretended she was my sister," Grandma said. "Because I always wanted a sister but never had one."

"I'm going to have a sister, aren't I?" Emma asked, suddenly remembering her mum.

"Of course you are, dear," Grandma said, and screwed up her face in an encouraging smile.

"It'll be great having someone to play with whenever I want," Emma said, curling up in a ball.

"She'll be too small to play to start with," Grandma reminded her.

"I know that." Emma thought that sometimes Grandma seemed to think *she* was a baby. "I'll help to look after her while she's little. When she's bigger, she'll be able to play games."

"That's right." Grandma tucked her in.

"When will I be able to see Mum?" Emma asked.

"It won't be long, I'm sure," Grandma said. She gave Emma a kiss and stroked her hair.

Grandma went to draw the curtains and looked out at the sky. There was a moon, but heavy, black clouds above the rooftops of the houses across the street were creeping nearer.

"The weather forecast said thunder," she told Emma. "It looks as if we're going to get some."

"Don't draw the curtains. Please, Grandma," Emma begged.

"You're not frightened of thunder, are you?"

"Of course not. I'm not a baby," Emma replied. "I like thunder and lightning. I think they're exciting."

"Well, all right," Grandma agreed. "I'll leave the curtains, but you try to go to sleep."

"I will. Goodnight, Grandma."

The Thunderstorm

Emma lay in bed and watched the line of clouds creep nearer. At last the moonlit patch of sky disappeared, and all was black. But on the bedroom ceiling was a pattern of shadows made by the street lights.

Emma waited for the thunder. Lying in bed watching rain on the window was something she enjoyed doing all by herself. It made her feel cosy and warm, and the thunder made her tingle with excitement. But all was quiet. The black clouds did nothing. Emma started to think about her mum.

She knew something was the matter. They could say everything was all right a thousand times, but they couldn't fool her. *She* knew when everyone was worried. They should tell her. She wasn't stupid. She wondered if her mum was ill. Then she wondered if the baby was ill. Could a baby be ill before it was born?

It wasn't fair not to tell her. Emma wanted to have a sister as much as Grandma wanted one when she was little. That was why she always said 'she' when she talked about the baby.

Emma and her mum had watched the baby growing. Her mum had got bigger and bigger. Most days after school while they were having a biscuit and drink, they had watched her mum's tummy together and seen the baby move. Her tummy would suddenly stick up in a little lump.

"I think that's her foot," her mum would say.

Then later Emma would say, "That lump's a bit big for a foot. I think it's her head. She must have turned a somersault."

"It felt like it," her mum would agree.

One day Emma had asked, "Will she look like me?"

"I expect so," her mum said, frowning. "Not as much like you as a twin sister would. But I expect she'll have blue eyes like you, because Daddy and I have blue eyes. And we've all got fairish hair, and we're not really fat, and we're not really thin..."

"We're not really tall, and we're not really short," Emma had added. "We're all in-between people."

"So I expect the baby will be the same as us," her mum had said.

"We're going to have an in-between baby," Emma had laughed.

Emma didn't know when she fell asleep, but suddenly she was awake again. Something had woken her up. For a second she couldn't think where she was. Then she remembered, she was staying at Grandma's. Nervously, she looked towards the window.

There was a flicker of light across the sky and a far-away rumble. She jumped – then laughed at herself. The thunderstorm had started. Was that what had woken her up? It must be very late, she thought. The street lights were out. She hadn't known they were turned off in the night.

Emma lay in bed frowning. There was something worrying her, but she couldn't remember what. She felt that it was really this worry, not the far-away thunder, which had woken her. What was it?

There was another distant flicker and a rumble. The room lit up again. That was when she remembered. She had left the wheelie-beelie outside the back door.

She listened carefully. The rain hadn't started yet. If she was quick, she could go downstairs and bring

her wheelie-beelie in before the big drops started to fall. She didn't need to wake Grandma or Grandpa. But she had to bring the wheelie-beelie into the house because the silvery wheels would go rusty if they got wet, and then they wouldn't work so well.

It was darker than she could ever remember. A flash of lightning showed her where the door was. She pushed back the blankets. At home she had a quilt. When her bare foot touched the floor she jumped.

The floor was icy cold. Slowly she stretched out her foot again. The floor was smooth and cold like the kitchen floor at home.

"Where's the carpet gone?" she asked out loud. When she went to bed there had been a green carpet with leaf patterns. She knew there had. She had followed the leaf stems lots of times to see where they went. But they never went anywhere, only round in loopy circles.

She felt about the cold floor by the bed with her foot until she found her slippers. She put them on as quickly as she could. That was warmer, but she still shivered as she stood up. She groped her way to the end of her bed. Her hand touched something hard like an iron bar. She slid her fingers over the cold surface.

"Oh, no," she said, and frowned to herself in the dark.

The bed was different. Her stomach seemed to pull itself tight. There were bars at the end of her bed like those she'd seen on brass beds in old pictures.

She put out her hand and touched the edge of the door. The light switch was near there. She spread out her fingers to search for it. They met a fat, round switch. She stopped.

Everything was different. When she had gone to bed, the switch had been square and flat. With one finger she flicked it. Nothing happened. Emma shivered again – she was frightened. For a second she thought of getting back into bed and hiding, but she wouldn't feel safe in a bed that had changed.

She groped for the door handle and turned it. The door creaked open. A brighter flash of lightning lit up the small landing at the top of the stairs. They were the same stairs she had come up to bed, but the carpet had gone and everywhere was shiny brown. The floor, the bannisters, the walls – they were all brown.

Emma started to tiptoe down. The dark was so thick it seemed to touch her. Why hadn't they left a light on? They always did. When she reached the bottom of the stairs, she bumped into a strange piece of furniture standing on the landing. A sudden, louder clap of thunder made her jump. The storm was creeping nearer. She wrapped her arms round herself to have something to hold onto.

Then she saw a pale, flickering light coming from the spare room where no-one slept.

She took a step forward. The door wasn't open wide enough to see inside. She pushed it very slowly. It swung silently back.

Everything was different. There was a big chest of drawers as tall as herself, a wooden wardrobe with a mirror on the door and carved patterns each side of it, and a thick, black curtain which hid the window. The light came from a short, fat candle which burned inside a little china church on the chest of drawers.

Emma's eyes rested on the bed. Lying there was a girl who looked about the same age as her.

"Who are you?" Emma asked, before she could stop herself.

The Wheelie-Beelie Bomb Race

The girl in the bed opened her eyes and looked at Emma. Then she banged her head on the pillow to make sure she was awake.

"Who are *you*?" she asked Emma.

"I asked first," Emma said.

"You're Emma," the girl said, her voice rising in surprise. "You're Emma. You really are."

"Who are *you*?" Emma asked again.

"I'm Polly, of course. What are you doing here?" Polly asked.

I ought to be asking that, Emma thought. But she answered all the same.

"I was going to put my wheelie-beelie away before the rain started when I saw your candle."

"It's a night-light," Polly told her.

"It looks like a candle," Emma argued.

"Candles are taller and thinner," Polly said, as if Emma was stupid for not knowing.

"I've never seen a candle night-light before," Emma said, "so I wouldn't know, would I? Mine just plugs in. Anyway, what are you doing here?"

"What do you mean?" Polly asked, sounding surprised. "I live here."

There was a sudden crash of thunder. The storm was suddenly very near.

"I must get my wheelie-beelie before it rains," Emma said quickly.

But Polly jumped out of bed.

"That's not thunder," she shouted. "It's bombs!"

"What?" Emma asked, not believing her ears.

"Bombs," Polly repeated, pulling on her dressing gown. She saw Emma's puzzled face. "Bombs," she said again. "The planes are dropping bombs. We must go in the shelter." She grabbed Emma's hand. "Come on, quick."

She blew out the night-light and dragged Emma onto the landing. She felt on top of the piece of furniture Emma had bumped into and found a torch.

Emma saw the beam of light from the torch bob along the landing and into her grandma and grandpa's bedroom. She stood still as she'd been told because she felt too lost to do anything else. She would have felt less lost in a completely strange house. Yet here she was in the house she had gone to sleep in a few hours ago, but it was all different. There was even a strange girl in it who didn't seem very surprised to see her.

She heard Polly's voice from the bedroom crying urgently, "Wake up, Mam. Wake up!"

"What is it?" a woman's voice asked sleepily.

"There's a raid," Polly's voice told her. "They're bombing us."

"I didn't hear the siren," the woman's voice said, suddenly awake.

"I don't think there's been a warning," Polly said. "The planes must have got through somehow."

Emma listened, not believing what she heard. Where was she? Everything was wrong. Just for a second, she felt again that she wanted to rush back up the stairs and hide in her bed.

Suddenly the house was shaken by three crashes of thunder which leap-frogged one another, each nearer than the last.

"Quick!" the woman's voice shouted. "Down to the shelter. Run! Go on – I'm coming."

The torch came darting back onto the landing. "Come on," Polly's voice said from behind the light. "Have you got your gas-mask?"

"What's a gas-mask?" Emma asked.

"Don't you know *anything*?" Polly yelled at her. "Oh, never mind." She caught hold of Emma's hand again and pulled her towards the stairs. "Come on, *run*."

The stairs were a dark tunnel. The girls plunged down them following the orange torch beam. At the bottom they turned into the back room. The carpet had disappeared in here, too, and Emma's slippers slapped on the cold floor. It was brown just like her bedroom.

35

"Why's everything brown?" she asked.

"What d'you mean?" Polly asked, slowing down.

"Why are the floors and the walls and the doors brown?" Emma asked again.

Polly shook her head. "I don't know. They just are. What else would they be?"

Emma was just about to put on a bored voice and recite a list of colours when the woman's voice came from the top of the stairs.

"What are you doing? Get a move on. I'll bring the blankets."

Polly ran into the kitchen. Emma felt by the door and found the light switch. It was metal again, like the one in her room. She flicked it down. This time a small bulb came on. There was another crash of thunder, and the light went dim then bright again.

Polly gave a cry. "Turn it off!" She flung herself across the room and hit the switch.

"Why d'you do that?" Emma demanded.

"The blackout," Polly said crossly, dragging her towards the back door. "If they see a light, they'll drop their bombs on it."

There were more thunderous crashes. They sounded even louder than before.

"Get in the shelter," Polly's mother yelled from behind them. "They're getting nearer." Polly jerked the door open and put out her torch at the same time.

"Where are we going?" Emma asked.

"The air-raid shelter – at the bottom of the garden," Polly shouted as they ran outside.

There was a flash like lightning, and for a moment Emma could see the garden as clearly as in the daytime. There was no pigeon coop or shed. In their place were neat rows of vegetables. The brick path was the same and led straight to her rockery mountain at the bottom of the garden.

But the rockery mountain had changed. It was still a rockery at the sides, but facing her was a doorway into the mountain.

"That's our shelter," Polly said.

In front of them stood Emma's wheelie-beelie, but now it had big pram wheels.

There was another crash. Then another, even nearer, that made them duck.

37

"Quick!" Polly screamed.

"Run!" her mother's voice came from behind them.

"Get on the wheelie-beelie," Emma shouted.

Polly jumped on. Emma gave it a push and leapt on behind.

They hurtled down the garden path with crashes

like thunder and flashes like lightning all around them. Emma dug her nails into the wood of the seat.

Crash! Crash! CRASH!

The last crash seemed to hurl itself out of the sky straight on top of them.

"Dive for the shelter!" Polly's mum screamed

from behind them.

The wheelie-beelie hit the first step down to the shelter, and Polly and Emma were flung off into the darkness. Polly's mother threw herself in after them. Emma was buried in the middle of people, dressing-gowns and blankets.

As they landed on the shelter floor, there came the most deafening roar she had ever heard. The whole world shook.

She struggled to escape, but was trapped.
Where was she? she asked herself.
How had she got here?

Grandma

Emma rolled about, trying to escape.

"Whatever's going on?" a distant voice asked.

Emma felt things being pulled off her. Bright light shone in her eyes.

"That's better," Grandma's voice said. "Now we can see which way is up."

Emma blinked and looked round. She was sitting on the floor by her bed in a pile of blankets. There was a green carpet with leaf patterns as usual, and her bed didn't have bars.

"Have you been having a bad dream?"

Grandma asked.

"It wasn't a dream," Emma said without thinking. "I was really there."

There was a rumble of thunder.

"The wheelie-beelie," Emma cried. "I must bring it in before it rains." She stood up.

"Don't worry about that," Grandma laughed. "Grandpa put it away before we went to bed."

Emma looked up at the window. Even with the bedroom light on she could see faint shadows from the street light on the ceiling.

"In the war," Emma asked, "were the street lights switched off?"

"What a thing to ask at this time of night," Grandma chuckled.

"Were they?" Emma repeated.

"Yes," Grandma agreed. "It was quite dark. We called it the blackout."

"I know," Emma said thoughtfully. "What was that brown shiny stuff people used to put on the floor instead of carpet? It was very cold if you put your feet on it."

"Whatever's brought all this on?" Grandma exclaimed. "I think you must mean lino."

"That's a funny word," Emma said, but she didn't laugh.

There was another rumble of thunder.

"We'll draw the curtains," Grandma said. "You hop back into bed. The storm must have woken you."

"It sounds like bombs," Emma said.

"What makes you say a thing like that?" Grandma asked in surprise.

"I've heard them," Emma told her.

"On television, I suppose," Grandma said, drawing the curtains.

"Were any bombs ever dropped near this house when you were a little girl?" Emma asked.

Grandma looked thoughtful. "There was *one* terrible night," she said. "We got no warning that the planes were coming. My mum and I were fast asleep. Dad was away in the army, of course. Something…" She stopped speaking for a second. "Something woke me up. We ran down to the shelter."

"In the rockery?" Emma asked.

"However did you know that?" Grandma asked. Emma didn't answer. "I suppose Grandpa told you. Anyway," Grandma went on, "all the windows in our house were broken – and do you know what? When I went back to my bedroom there was a huge piece of glass like a sword sticking right through my blankets. It was lucky I had got out of bed in time."

"What's a gas-mask?" Emma asked.

"No more questions," Grandma said. "Go back to sleep." She straightened Emma's bed. "It's the middle of the night."

Grandma went over to the door. "Snuggle down and go to sleep," she said, and switched off the light.

Emma could still see her because the landing light was on.

"I bet," Emma said softly, "I bet I can guess the name of your secret friend."

"No more games," Grandma said.

"She was called Emma, like me. Wasn't she?"

Grandma pretended not to have heard. But Emma could tell that she had. Just for a second Grandma's face had a funny-worried look.

Then she turned and went downstairs without saying anything.

Emma lay in bed and thought about what had happened. She must have had a dream — but it hadn't felt like a dream. It had all been so real. The house, the bombs, Polly.

Am I, Emma wondered, really Grandma's secret friend?

Grandma had nearly said something after tea about when her secret friend had been real. Had that been the night of the bombs, when her secret friend had woken her up and saved her life?

Emma felt sure it was. But the girl had said that her name was Polly, and Grandma's name wasn't Polly. That was only what Grandpa said when he wanted his tea. Polly put the kettle on. It was all very puzzling. Emma fell asleep still wondering.

Polly Again

Emma's dad arrived the next morning while she was having breakfast.

"I've got some news," he announced, as he came in.

"The baby," Emma cried, jumping up and running to him.

"How would you like a baby sister?" he asked, lifting her up and swinging her round.

"Oh, I wanted a sister. I wanted a sister," Emma chanted happily.

Grandpa shook hands with her dad, smiled and said, "Congratulations!"

Grandma asked, "How is she?" and Emma knew that she meant her mum, and that they *had* been worried about something.

"What was the matter before?" Emma asked.

"Nothing really," her dad told her. "The baby was a bit late coming. That was all."

"I knew something was the matter," Emma said. "You should have told me. I'm not a baby."

"Perhaps we should have," her dad said quietly, "but we didn't think you'd understand."

"Well, I would have," Emma said.

"Yes, I think you would have." Her dad gave her another kiss. "I'll tell you what," he said. "You can choose the baby's name."

Emma thought. There was only one possible

name for a real sister for her to play with.

"Polly," Emma said. "Her name is Polly."

"That's short for Pauline," Grandma said. "That's my name. Did you know?"

"Were you called Polly when you were little?" Emma asked.

"When I was your age I was called Polly," her grandma said.

"All right," Emma's dad said to her. "We'll name her Pauline after Grandma and you can call her Polly."

"When she's older," Emma said, "I'll give her a ride on my wheelie-beelie."

Emma watched Grandma's face as she said that. It had the funny-worried look she'd seen in the middle of the night. Emma was quiet for a moment, thinking.

What had happened last night was something to do with the wheelie-beelie. She felt sure that somehow it had helped her to save Grandma's life. She had woken up because in her sleep she had been worried about the wheelie-beelie getting wet. Then she had woken Polly up and they had gone downstairs before the bomb had smashed Polly's bedroom window. After that they had ridden the wheelie-beelie together, and it had brought her back again – like a time machine. A wheelie-beelie time machine.

She wondered again if it could all have been a

dream. But it had seemed too real for that. She sighed. Whatever had happened, she had a little sister and everything was all right.

"What does the baby look like?" Emma asked.

"When she was born, she was all purple," her dad said.

"What?" Emma exclaimed. "I've never heard of a purple baby."

"She is a very big baby as well," her dad went on.

"Does she have fairish hair like me?" Emma asked.

47

"No. Her hair is quite dark." Her dad smiled.

"She's supposed to be an in-between baby," Emma said, "like the rest of us. But still, it doesn't matter. I've got a new sister and that's the important thing."

The other important thing, Emma thought, is that if ever there was anything the matter again, her mum and dad would tell her all about it.